Dog Groups

Sporting Group

by Julie Murray

2

Dash!
LEVELED READERS
An Imprint of Abdo Zoom • abdobooks.com

Dash!
LEVELED READERS

Level 1 – Beginning
Short and simple sentences with familiar words or patterns for children who are beginning to understand how letters and sounds go together.

Level 2 – Emerging
Longer words and sentences with more complex language patterns for readers who are practicing common words and letter sounds.

Level 3 – Transitional
More developed language and vocabulary for readers who are becoming more independent.

THIS BOOK CONTAINS RECYCLED MATERIALS

abdobooks.com

Published by Abdo Zoom, a division of ABDO, PO Box 398166, Minneapolis, Minnesota 55439.

Printed in the United States of America, North Mankato, Minnesota.
102023
012024

Photo Credits: Getty Images, Shutterstock
Production Contributors: Jennie Forsberg, Grace Hansen
Design Contributors: Candice Keimig, Neil Klinepier

Library of Congress Control Number: 2023938008

Publisher's Cataloging in Publication Data

Names: Murray, Julie, author.
Title: Sporting group / by Julie Murray
Description: Minneapolis, Minnesota : Abdo Zoom, 2024 | Series: Dog groups | Includes online resources and index.
Identifiers: ISBN 9781098284046 (lib. bdg.) | ISBN 9781098284763 (eBook) | ISBN 9781098285128 (Read-to-Me eBook)
Subjects: LCSH: Sporting dogs--Juvenile literature. | Hunting dogs--Juvenile literature. | Dog sports--Juvenile literature. | Dogs--Juvenile literature. | Dogs--Behavior--Juvenile literature.
Classification: DDC 636.75--dc23

Table of Contents

Sporting Group

The Sporting Group has more than 30 dog **breeds**. It is one of the original dog groups of the American Kennel Club (AKC).

German Wirehaired Pointer

Golden Retriever

Dogs in this group were **bred** to work with hunters. They help locate or retrieve game.

There are four types of dogs in the Sporting Group.

Setter

Spaniel

Characteristics

Sporting dogs like to be active. They have a lot of energy!

Labrador Retriever

Irish Setter

They love the outdoors.
They have good **instincts**
on land and in the water.

English Springer Spaniel

Sporting dogs are easy to train. They enjoy retrieving and field exercises.

Many sporting dogs have a water-repellent coat. This special coat keeps them warm and safe.

German Shorthaired Pointer

Sporting dogs are loving and loyal. They make great family pets.

English Cocker Spaniel

Some are good **therapy dogs**. Others work as search and rescue dogs.

More Sporting Breeds

Barbet

Brittany

English Setter

Gordon Setter

Vizsla

Weimaraner

Glossary

bred – developed over time for a certain purpose.

breed – a particular type of animal.

instinct – natural behavior in an animal that is not taught but is simply part of what the animal is born with.

therapy dog – a dog that is trained to provide affection, comfort, and support to people.

Index

Online Resources

Booklinks
NONFICTION NETWORK
FREE! ONLINE NONFICTION RESOURCES

To learn more about the Sporting Group, please visit **abdobooklinks.com** or scan this QR code. These links are routinely monitored and updated to provide the most current information available.